COUNTRIES

JAPAN

R.L. Van

Big Buddy Books
An Imprint of Abdo Publishing
abdobooks.com

abdobooks.com

Published by Abdo Publishing, a division of ABDO, PO Box 398166, Minneapolis, Minnesota 55439.
Copyright © 2023 by Abdo Consulting Group, Inc. International copyrights reserved in all countries. No part of this book may be reproduced in any form without written permission from the publisher. Big Buddy Books™ is a trademark and logo of Abdo Publishing.

Printed in the United States of America, North Mankato, Minnesota
102022
012023

THIS BOOK CONTAINS
RECYCLED MATERIALS

Design: Emily O'Malley, Mighty Media, Inc.
Production: Mighty Media, Inc.
Editor: Jessica Rusick
Cover Photograph: chanchai duangdoosan/Shutterstock Images
Interior Photographs: Aeypix/Shutterstock Images, p. 27 (bottom); Anthony Shaw Photography/Shutterstock Images, p. 27 (top left); asiangrandkid/Shutterstock Images, p. 26 (left); beeboys/Shutterstock Images, p. 6 (bottom); Blue Planet Studio/Shutterstock Images, p. 6 (top); cowardlion/Shutterstock Images, p. 6 (middle); Dane Gillett/Shutterstock Images, p. 17; Dave Hansche/Shutterstock Images, p. 15; Denis Makarenko/Shutterstock Images, p. 21; Everett Collection/Shutterstock Images, p. 29 (top left); f11photo/Shutterstock Images, p. 25; Fly_and_Dive/Shutterstock Images, p. 29 (bottom); Lance Cpl. Achilles Tsantarliotis/Wikimedia Commons, p. 29 (top right); Leonard Zhukovsky/Shutterstock Images, p. 23; leungchopan/Shutterstock Images, p. 19; lukulo/iStockphoto, pp. 5 (compass), 7 (compass); National Diet Library/Wikimedia Commons, p. 9; Pyty/Shutterstock Images, p. 5 (map); roihun matpor/Shutterstock Images, p. 30 (flag); Ruslan Maiborodin/Shutterstock Images, p. 7 (map); Sakarin Sawasdinaka/Shutterstock Images, p. 30 (currency); Tatohra/Shutterstock Images, p. 13; Travel Stock/Shutterstock Images, p. 26 (right); Wikimedia Commons, pp. 11, 27 (top right), 28
Design Elements: Mighty Media, Inc.
Country population and area figures taken from the CIA World Factbook

Library of Congress Control Number: 2022940521

Publisher's Cataloging-in-Publication Data
Names: Van, R.L., author.
Title: Japan / by R.L. Van
Description: Minneapolis, Minnesota : Abdo Publishing, 2023 | Series: Countries | Includes online resources and index.
Identifiers: ISBN 9781532199677 (lib. bdg.) | ISBN 9781098274870 (ebook)
Subjects: LCSH: Japan--Juvenile literature. | Asia--Juvenile literature. | Japan--History--Juvenile literature. | Geography--Juvenile literature.
Classification: DDC 952--dc23

CONTENTS

PASSPORT TO JAPAN

Japan is a country in the Pacific Ocean. It is made up of many islands off the eastern coast of Asia. More than 124 million people live there.

DID YOU KNOW?

Japanese words are drawn with symbols or characters to represent sounds.

WHERE IS JAPAN?
N
W E
S
Russia
China
Sea of Japan
Hokkaido
North Korea
South Korea
Honshu
JAPAN
Shikoku
Kyushu
Pacific Ocean

IMPORTANT CITIES

Tokyo is Japan's **capital** and largest **metropolitan area**. It is a center of business and art.

Osaka is Japan's second-largest metropolitan area. It is known for its businesses, food, and entertainment.

Nagoya is Japan's third-largest metropolitan area. It has many car factories.

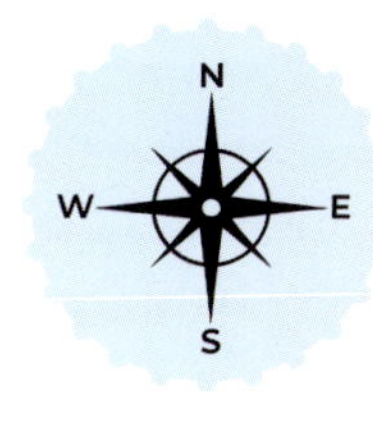

N
W
E
S

DID YOU KNOW?

Some Japanese cities have underground shopping areas because there is limited land for building.

JAPAN

Nagoya
Population: 9.57 million

Tokyo
Population: 37.27 million

Osaka
Population: 19.06 million

SAY IT

Tokyo
TOH-kee-oh

Osaka
oh-SAH-kah

Nagoya
nah-GOY-ah

JAPAN IN HISTORY

The first people to settle in Japan were hunters and gatherers. Around 600, Japan began to use ideas from China. These included **Buddhism** and writing. Throughout history, Japanese families fought for power. Around 1100, warriors called samurai became powerful.

Samurai were employed by wealthy families to protect their land and riches.

In 1192, military **dictators** called shoguns took power. In the 1600s, they isolated Japan from other countries. In 1867, shogun rule ended. Emperor Meiji took power and created new government systems. Japan quickly became a powerful, modern country. It suffered much in **World War II**. But the country worked hard to rebuild.

Japan's first shogun was
Minamoto Yoritomo.

AN IMPORTANT SYMBOL

Japan's flag has a red circle on a white background. The country is a **parliamentary constitutional monarchy**. The prime minister leads the government. A group called the Diet makes laws. Japan has an emperor. But he has little power.

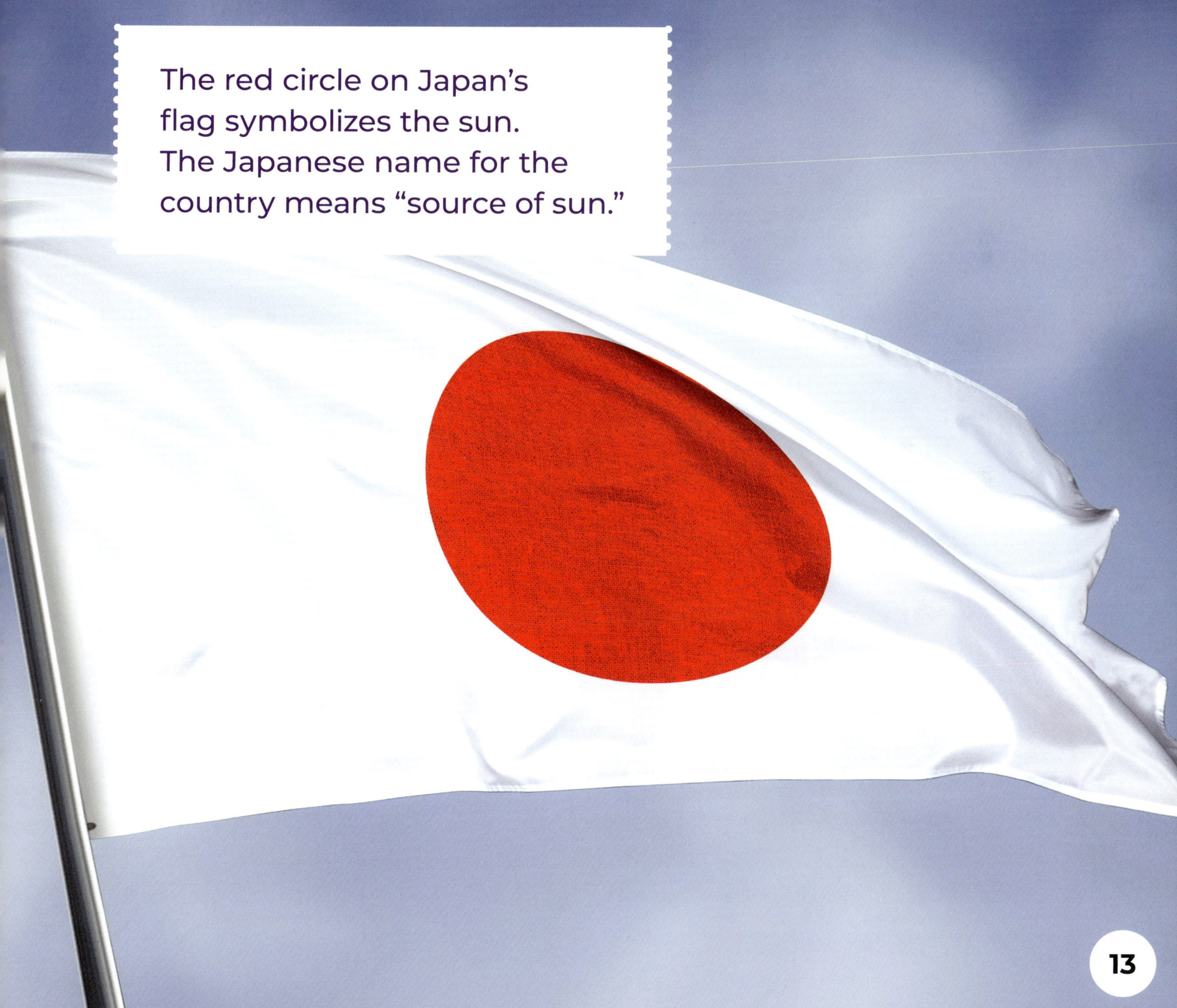

The red circle on Japan's flag symbolizes the sun. The Japanese name for the country means "source of sun."

ACROSS THE LAND

Japan has mountains, forests, rivers, and lakes. It has more than 100 active **volcanoes**. Up to 2,000 **earthquakes** occur in Japan yearly.

Japanese black bears, wild boars, and macaques live in Japan. Trees, flowers, and bamboo grow there.

SAY IT

macaque
muh-KAK

Japanese macaques are called "snow monkeys" because they live in snowy climates.

EARNING A LIVING

Japan is known for manufacturing and trade. Factory workers make cars, ships, and electronics. Many people have service jobs. They may work for banks or the government.

Japan is a world leader in fishing. Farmers mainly grow rice. Some grow soybeans, wheat, potatoes, or tea.

In 2018, Japan's fisheries caught 4.2 million tons of fish.

LIFE IN JAPAN

Sushi, tempura, and rice are common Japanese foods. Popular sports include sumo wrestling, baseball, and soccer. Many Japanese people are **Buddhist** or **Shinto**. People celebrate these religions at traditional festivals.

DID YOU KNOW?

Students in Japan attend school year-round. Some have classes on weekends.

Tempura is battered and deep-fried seafood, meat, or vegetables.

19

FAMOUS FACES

Hayao Miyazaki was born in Tokyo in 1941. He enjoyed **manga** and animation when he was young. In 1985, he and other animators founded Studio Ghibli. There, Miyazaki directed many successful films. They include *My Neighbor Totoro* and *Spirited Away*.

Hayao Miyazaki loves flying. Many of his movies feature airplanes and flight!

Naomi Osaka was born in Osaka, Japan, in 1997. Her father taught her to play tennis when she was young. Osaka began playing tennis professionally in 2013. She has won four Grand Slam titles. She also lit the Olympic cauldron at the Tokyo 2020 Olympics.

Naomi Osaka's mother is from Japan. Her father is from Haiti.

A GREAT COUNTRY

Japan has beautiful land and a rich history and culture. The people and places of Japan help make the world a more interesting place.

Kyoto is known for its temples, shrines, and gardens. The city is called the "cultural capital" of Japan.

If you ever visit Japan, here are some places to go and things to do!

DISCOVER

Meet characters like Hello Kitty at the Sanrio Puroland theme park.

CELEBRATE

Attend a cherry blossom festival. These festivals celebrate the blooming of cherry blossom trees in the spring.

REMEMBER

Visit Peace Memorial Park in Hiroshima. The city was destroyed by an **atomic bomb** in **World War II**.

CHEER

Watch a baseball game at the Tokyo Dome. The Yomiuri Giants often play there.

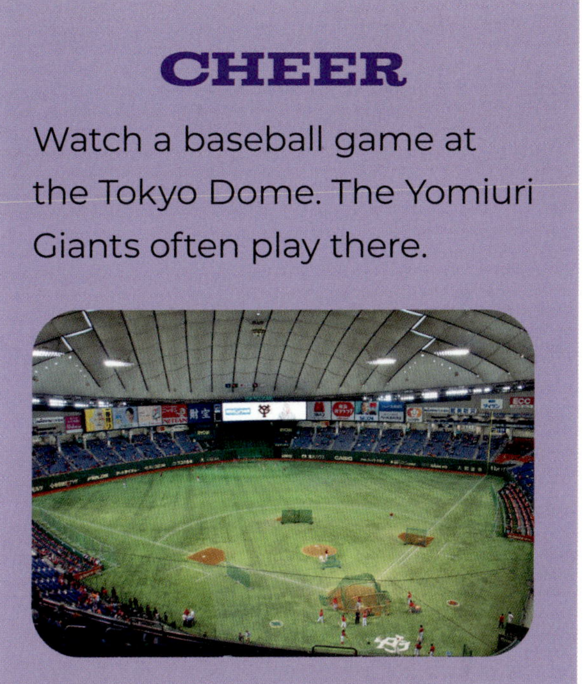

EXPLORE

Visit the **volcano** Mount Fuji, Japan's tallest peak.

TIMELINE

794

Heian-kyo became Japan's **capital**. It was later called Kyoto.

1192

The first shogun began ruling Japan.

1858

Japan signed a treaty reopening trade to the United States. It opened trade to many other countries after this too.

1868

Tokyo became Japan's capital.

1945

The United States dropped **atomic bombs** on Hiroshima and Nagasaki (*pictured*). This killed more than 100,000 people. It led to the end of **World War II**.

2019

Emperor Akihito (*pictured*) became the first emperor to give up the throne since 1817. His son Naruhito became emperor.

2011

A large **earthquake** caused a **tsunami**. Thousands of people died in this disaster.

JAPAN
UP CLOSE

Official Name
Nippon or Nihon (Japan)

Flag

Population
124,214,766 (2022 est.)
11th-most-populated country

Total Area
145,914 square miles
(377,915 sq km)
62nd-largest country

Official Language
Japanese

Capital
Tokyo

Currency
Yen

Form of Government
Parliamentary
constitutional
monarchy

National Anthem
"Kimigayo" ("The
Emperor's Reign")

GLOSSARY

atomic bomb (uh-TAH-mihk BAHM)—a very powerful bomb that uses the energy of atoms. Atoms are tiny particles that make up matter.

Buddhism (BOO-dih-zuhm)—a religion based on the teachings of the Buddha. Something related to Buddhism is Buddhist.

capital—a city where government leaders meet.

dictator—a ruler with complete control who often governs in a cruel way.

earthquake (UHRTH-kwayk)—a shaking of a part of the earth.

manga—a Japanese comic book or graphic novel.

metropolitan area—a large city and its surrounding cities and suburbs.

parliamentary constitutional monarchy—a form of government in which a parliament makes the laws. The monarch has only those powers given by a country's laws and constitution.

Shinto—a Japanese religion in which people worship ancestors and nature gods.

tsunami (soo-NAH-mee)—a group of powerful ocean waves that can destroy areas.

volcano—a deep opening in Earth's surface from which hot liquid rock or steam comes out.

World War II—a war fought in Europe, Asia, and Africa from 1939 to 1945.

ONLINE RESOURCES

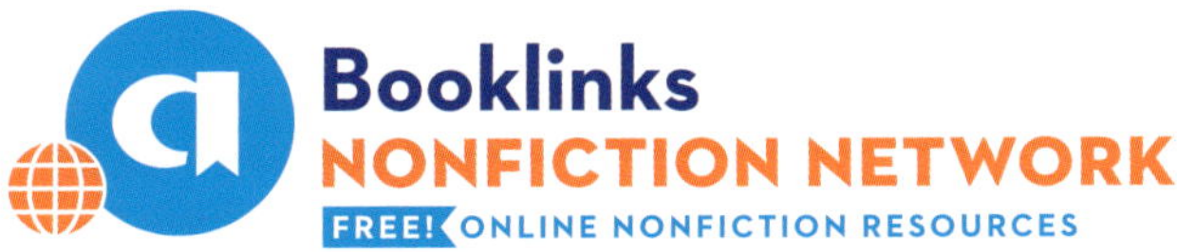

To learn more about Japan, please visit **abdobooklinks.com** or scan this QR code. These links are routinely monitored and updated to provide the most current information available.

INDEX